Stress
and Tension

CAUSES & EFFECTS OF EMOTIONS

CAUSES & EFFECTS OF EMOTIONS

Stress and Tension

Rosa Waters

Mason Crest

Mason Crest
450 Parkway Drive, Suite D
Broomall, PA 19008
www.masoncrest.com

Printed and bound in the United States of America.

First printing
9 8 7 6 5 4 3 2 1

Series ISBN: 978-1-4222-3067-1
ISBN: 978-1-4222-3079-4
ebook ISBN: 978-1-4222-8772-9

The Library of Congress has cataloged the
hardcopy format(s) as follows:
            Library of Congress Cataloging-in-Publication Data

Waters, Rosa, 1957-
  Stress and tension / Rosa Waters.
      pages cm. — (Causes & effects of emotions)
  Includes index.
  Audience: Age 12+
  Audience: Grade 7 to 8.
  ISBN 978-1-4222-3079-4 (hardback) — ISBN 978-1-4222-3067-1 (series)
— ISBN 978-1-4222-8772-9 (ebook) 1. Stress in adolescence—Juvenile literature. 2. Stress in children--Juvenile literature. 3. Stress (Psychology—Juvenile literature. 4. Stress management—Juvenile literature. I. Title.
  BF724.3.S86W38 2015
  155.9'042—dc23
                                            2014004385

CONTENTS

KEY ICONS TO LOOK FOR:

 Text-Dependent Questions: These questions send the reader back to the text for more careful attention to the evidence presented there.

 Words to Understand: These words with their easy-to-understand definitions will increase the reader's understanding of the text, while building vocabulary skills.

 Series Glossary of Key Terms: This back-of-the book glossary contains terminology used throughout this series. Words found here increase the reader's ability to read and comprehend higher-level books and articles in this field.

 Research Projects: Readers are pointed toward areas of further inquiry connected to each chapter. Suggestions are provided for projects that encourage deeper research and analysis.

 Sidebars: This boxed material within the main text allows readers to build knowledge, gain insights, explore possibilities, and broaden their perspectives by weaving together additional information to provide realistic and holistic perspectives.

INTRODUCTION

The journey of self-discovery for young adults can be a passage that includes times of introspection as well joyful experiences. It can also be a complicated route filled with confusing road signs and hazards along the way. The choices teens make will have lifelong impacts. From early romantic relationships to complex feelings of anxiousness, loneliness, and compassion, this series of books is designed specifically for young adults, tackling many of the challenges facing them as they navigate the social and emotional world around and within them. Each chapter explores the social emotional pitfalls and triumphs of young adults, using stories in which readers will see themselves reflected.

Adolescents encounter compound issues today in home, school, and community. Many young adults may feel ill equipped to identify and manage the broad range of emotions they experience as their minds and bodies change and grow. They face many adult problems without the knowledge and tools needed to find satisfactory solutions. Where do they fit in? Why are they afraid? Do others feel as lonely and lost as they do? How do they handle the emotions that can engulf them when a friend betrays them or they fail to make the grade? These are all important questions that young adults may face. Young adults need guidance to pilot their way through changing feelings that are influenced by peers, family relationships, and an ever-changing world. They need to know that they share common strengths and pressures with their peers. Realizing they are not alone with their questions can help them develop important attributes of resilience and hope.

The books in this series skillfully capture young people's everyday, real-life emotional journeys and provides practical and meaningful information that can offer hope to all who read them.

It covers topics that teens may be hesitant to discuss with others, giving them a context for their own feelings and relationships. It is an essential tool to help young adults understand themselves and their place in the world around them—and a valuable asset for teachers and counselors working to help young people become healthy, confident, and compassionate members of our society.

Cindy Croft, M.A.Ed
Director of the Center for Inclusive Child Care at Concordia University

Words to Understand

categories: Classes or groups that we sort things into.
negative: Bad; having to do with the downside of things.
inspire: Motivate you to do something positive.
psychologists: Experts who study the mind and emotions.
evolving: Slowly developing over many generations.
dilated: Got bigger or expanded.
chronic: Lasting for a long time.
nutrition: The parts of what you eat and drink that your body uses to function correctly.
ulcers: Sores on the inside of your stomach.
immune systems: The parts of your body that work together to fight off diseases.
anxiety: A long-lasting feeling of worry or fear.
depression: A feeling of sadness or hopeless, which can last for a long time.
destructive: Hurting something or someone.

ONE

WHAT ARE STRESS AND TENSION?

Jenna stared at her planner. She had two big papers due this week, one in history and one in English class. Her final exams for both science and math classes were this week too. And on top of all that, she had to get ready for her mom's birthday party on Saturday—*plus* her aunt and uncle and her little cousins would be visiting for the next few days. Jenna was good at writing papers, and she was pretty sure she could get at least a B on math test, and probably an A on her science exam. She was excited about throwing her mom a birthday party, and she loved spending time with her relatives, especially her cute little cousins. So why did she feel so desperate and overwhelmed as she looked at the week ahead?

"You'll be fine," her best friend Abby told her. "You're just stressed out. Relax! By next week, it will all be over and you'll be feeling great."

Feeling as though there's just too much life to fit into the time we have is one cause of stress.

WHEN THERE'S TOO MUCH LIFE

When we talk about "stress," we're referring to the feeling we get when we wonder whether we can cope with all the things life is asking us to handle. Anything that poses a challenge to our well-being can cause us stress (like a serious illness, a death, or a divorce in the family)—and even good things (getting a new pet, starting a new job, moving to a new home, or going to college) can cause stress as well. When lots of little things come at once (like schoolwork and family responsibilities all piling up in the same week), they can cause stress and tension as well.

Stress is a normal and natural part of life. We all experience it. When we do, we often speak of feeling "tense," as though we can't relax. We feel nervous. We may get upset easily. Life seems to be coming at us too fast. There's just too much of it! Our emotions feel overwhelmed. People often use the word to "tension" to describe a more short-term feeling like this, while they think of "stress" as something that lasts for a longer period of time. Psychologists and scientists, however, use the term to "stress" to describe a condition that affects both our emotions and our bodies. And really, these experts tell us, our emotions and our bodies can't be separated!

THE FEELINGS INSIDE OUR BRAINS

Our emotions are the feelings we have inside our minds. We've been experiencing them our entire life, ever since we were babies. Sometimes we feel happy, and sometimes we feel sad; sometime we feel angry, sometimes we're scared, and sometimes we are bored. All these feelings come and go inside us.

We may feel as though our inside feelings are telling us about outside reality. So when we feel sad, we may believe that the world really is a dreary place where bad things happen. We believe our sadness tells us something about the outside world. Actually, though, our sadness tells us more about ourselves and how we are responding to the outside world.

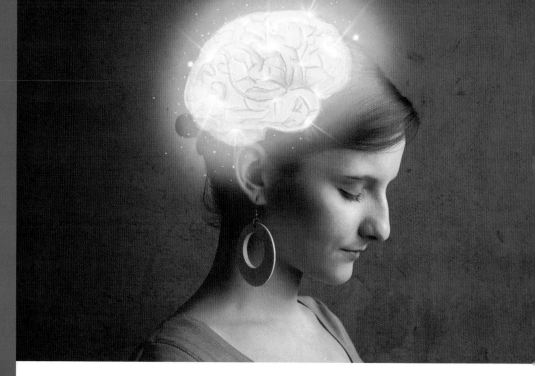

Your emotions are produced by things going on inside your brain.

Emotions take place inside our brains. That's why we can't separate them from the rest of our bodies—because emotions take place *inside* the body and they affect the entire body. These feelings are caused by chemical reactions and the way our brain cells communicate with each other. Different kinds of situations in the outside world will trigger different reactions within our brains. Each brain reaction feels a little different.

As very young children, we learned to give those brain feelings names at the same time we were learning to talk. We started out with very simple and basic **categories** for our emotions—happy and sad. Pretty soon we probably added "angry" and "scared" to our vocabularies. As we grew older, we learned more and more words to describe many shades of feeling. By now, we take those feelings for granted. They're just part of life.

Emotions have important jobs in our lives. They point our attention toward things that need our attention. When something

Make Connections

- Experts say that people feel only 6 main emotions—happiness, surprise, fear, sadness, disgust, and anger—and that all the other emotions we experience are some sort of combination or variation of these.
- There are more than 600 words in the English language used to describe emotions.
- We use 42 muscles in our faces to express emotions.

makes us happy, for example, our brains say, "Notice this! Try to get more of this in your life!" On the other hand, when something makes us sad or angry, our emotions tell us, "Do something! Try to change this situation!" Or when something scares us, the reaction in our brains tells us, "Be careful!"

When we were young children, all of us learned from our emotions. We learned what made us happy and what made us sad, what scared us and what made us laugh. We learned to change our behavior in response. Positive emotions—like joy and excitement and love—give us the energy we need to make friends, be creative, and do cool things. *Negative* feelings—like grief and anger and fear—aren't all bad either. They teach us to stay way from things that might hurt us, and they can *inspire* us to try to change our circumstances. They let our friends and family know when we need help.

Stress isn't actually a single emotion so much as a combination of many emotions and physical feelings. It's the way our bodies respond when too many demands are being placed on us.

FIGHT OR FLIGHT

When we're facing many demands from life, our bodies automatically go into what scientists and *psychologists* call the

In a situation like this, you have to decide: are you going to fight—or run away?

"fight-or-flight response." This response is the body's natural reaction to a challenge.

When this response was **evolving**, thousands and thousands of years ago, danger was something that had to be either fought or run away from. If your long-ago ancestor was facing an angry bear, for example, he had to either attack it and kill it—or run away from it as fast as he could. As a result, his brain sent out messages to the rest of his body, getting him ready to either fight or run away. His heart beat harder, and he breathed faster, sending more oxygen to his muscles. His digestion slowed down, while his blood pressure increased, so that more blood could go to the muscles in his arms and legs. His pupils **dilated** so he could see better. His muscles tensed, getting him ready to *move*.

In today's world, danger is often not quite as simple—but our bodies don't know that. They still get ready for fight or flight, the same way human bodies have been doing for thousands and thousands of years.

When stress doesn't last very long, that reaction can help you deal with whatever's coming at you. Jenna's fight-or-flight response to stress may feel uncomfortable, but it will probably help her get through her busy week. The fight-or-flight response will also help you deal with an emergency. That's what it's made for.

TOO MUCH STRESS

Your body responds to a crisis with a flood of brain chemicals that trigger changes throughout your body. Once the crisis is over, the brain and the rest of the body go back to normal. Your prehistoric ancestor either killed the bear or escaped from it safely. The fight-or-flight response wasn't designed to continue for long periods of time. It was meant for short periods. That bear didn't chase your ancestor for the next six months!

In today's world, though, we talk about *chronic* stress. It doesn't go away. Sometimes, life just keeps coming at us, presenting us with seemingly endless challenges. In Jenna's case, her busy week will be over, and her life will go back to normal—but what if it didn't? What if instead, the next week her mother was in a car accident and had to go into the hospital? And then the next week Jenna's father got seriously sick, so that Jenna had to take over many of the responsibilities around the house while her parents recovered. Now she's trying to juggle school and housework, along with her fear and worry about her parents' health. Then, just as her parents start to get better, her mother finds out that her employer has transferred her to a different city. The family is going to have to move. Jenna's life is just one challenge after another—and her stress level never goes down. She feels tense and overwhelmed all the time.

Chronic stress like this can create problems for us. The brain chemicals that are so good at getting our bodies ready to fight or run away aren't so good for long-term situations. They can make our digestive systems not work the way they're supposed to, so that we either eat too much and gain weight—or eat too little and don't get the **nutrition** our bodies need to be healthy. The tension we're experiencing can make our stomachs produce too much acid, giving us stomachaches. If this goes on too long, we might get **ulcers** or develop some other painful condition in our digestive system. Stress reactions can also make our **immune systems** not work as well, so we're more likely to get sick more often (which, of course, will probably add to the tension we're feeling!). Too much stress can also upset the balance of chemicals within our brains, causing mental disorders like **anxiety** and **depression**. And on top of all that, we may not be able to sleep very well. The fight-or-flight response is meant to make us more alert than usual, so that we can deal with danger—but that extra alertness is a bad thing when it goes on day after day. Our bodies and brains need sleep in order to heal themselves and function normally, so not sleeping just makes worse all the other problems that go along with chronic stress.

Sometimes, even good things can cause stress. Imagine you have a new boyfriend or girlfriend, you landed an after-school job you were hoping to get, and you're taking a really challenging class with your favorite teacher. All those circumstances are things you were really hoping would happen. In fact, your life couldn't be better! So why do you feel so tense and stressed?

Your body can't really tell the difference between "bad" and "good" things in your life. It just knows that you're being faced with more demands on your time. It's trying to help you juggle the excitement of a new romance alongside the responsibilities of a new job, combined with lots of hard homework. From your body's perspective, it's not that much different from what Abby's been going through.

MODERN-DAY STRESS

People talk a lot about stress these days. It's a big problem for a lot of people. You might get the impression that it's a new problem. People often talk as though stress is a modern problem that

Make Connections

Scientists know that mammals, birds, and reptiles all experience many of the same fight-or-flight reactions humans do in response to danger. Animals' brains send out signals that increase breathing, speed up heart rate, increase blood pressure, increase the liver's ability to pump sugar into the bloodstream, and open up blood vessels in the large muscles to maximize the delivery of nutrients and oxygen. All these reactions take place in humans too. These physical responses make sure that the animal has lots of fuel in its blood, that it has a more forceful heart to pump the blood around, that its muscles are working at their best possible levels. Say you're a rabbit running away from a fox: these body changes are exactly what you need to avoid becoming a meal!

Animals can also face chronic stress, such as hunger during periods when there's less food or pain from an infection or injury. Animals have evolved ways that allow their bodies cope with both pain and starvation. These physical responses give them a fighting chance to get back on their feet and survive. For humans, stress seems like a bad thing—but it actually serves a similar function. It's a survival mechanism.

people didn't experience a long time ago, back in the "good old days" when life was simpler.

Certainly, modern-day stress is different. Your grandparents didn't have people texting them every hour of the day. They probably weren't expected to study lots of complicated subjects when they were in school. Their schedules probably weren't as jam packed with after-school activities as yours is.

But people have always experienced stress. And ours today isn't so bad if you compare it to what your long-long-ago ancestors faced. Think about it. What would you rather have to face: a

Research Project

This chapter says that humans have always experienced stress, even though the stressors may have been different a hundred or a thousand years ago. Research the life of a typical person your age in an earlier historical era, and describe the sources of stress that person would have faced. What was expected of a person your age during that era? What were his or her responsibilities? What dangers did that person face? Compare and contrast the stress this individual faced with the stress you encounter in your life today.

really tough semester at school—or a long winter of near starvation? A bad case of the flu—or most of your entire community being wiped out in a war with another tribe? Even a hundred years ago, kids your age were facing plenty of stress. On top of going to school, they may have been responsible for lots of hard work on a farm. They may have been expected to get married and start raising a family before they were twenty. Sickness was common, and many diseases didn't have medicine yet to treat them. Life wasn't that easy.

Meanwhile, in the past, people had little understanding of what was going on inside their bodies. They tried to make sense out of what was happening in their world by relying on superstition and religion. Otherwise, they would have felt as though they had no control over life.

COPING WITH STRESS

People today still need to feel as though they have some control over life. Many of us still rely on faith in God or in some other higher order to help us cope with the challenges we face. We may also have superstitions we believe are true—and that may

Text-Dependent Questions

1. Explain what emotions are, according to this chapter. Where do they take place and what is their purpose?

2. Describe the fight-or-flight response. How does it affect the body? What is its purpose?

3. Define the word "chronic" as it's used in this chapter.

4. What physical reactions do animals experience when faced with danger that indicate they may experience some of the same stress reactions humans do?

not be a bad thing! Anything that strengthens our sense of control can help us emotionally deal with stress.

Sometimes, though, we rely on unhealthy ways to deal with life's normal stress and tension. Abusing drugs and alcohol is an example of this. So is eating too much—or really, doing *anything* too much, whether it's exercising or playing video games. Anything that's done too much can become **destructive**, both to our bodies and to our lives.

Stress has been a part of human experience for thousands of years. Today, though, scientists understand a lot more about what's going on during this normal human reaction. And the more *you* understand what's going on inside your body when you're stressed, the more you can learn to work with your body. You'll feel a little more in control.

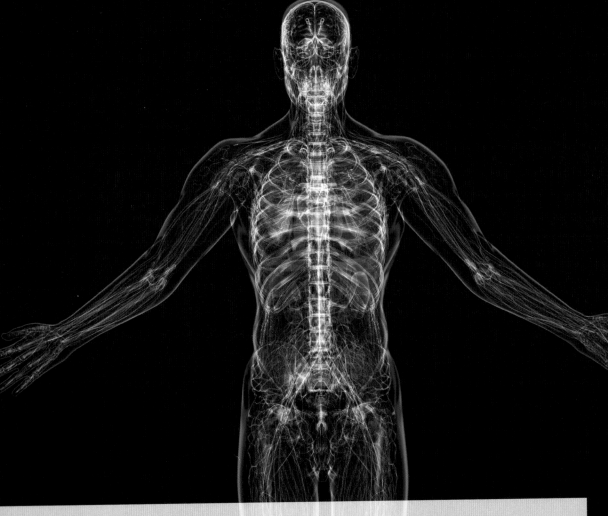

Words to Understand

activates: Switches on; causes to start working.
aggression: Anger or being ready to attack.
researchers: Scientists who try to discover new things or learn more about a certain thing.
stroke: A blocked or burst blood vessel inside your brain.
susceptibility: Likelihood that a person will be affected by something.
interpersonal: Having to do with the relationships between people.
genetics: The characteristics of the DNA a person inherited from his parents.

TWO

WHAT'S THE CONNECTION TO OUR BRAINS AND BODIES?

Think about Jenna's situation in the last chapter. At first glance, it seems as though stress is coming at her from *outside*, from the world around her. Actually, however, stress is something that's happening *inside* Jenna. Although it was triggered by her external circumstances, it's her internal response that's making her feel tense and stressed out.

Stress **activates** certain regions of the brain, the same areas that control eating, **aggression**, and your body's immune response. It switches on the same nerve circuits that would respond if you were facing a life-threatening danger. These reactions evolved to help our ancestors deal with sudden dangers without having to sit down and think up with a plan. Their bodies just reacted automatically, right away, without them having to waste time thinking about it.

Today, your stress reaction is more likely to be called on to

STRESS AND TENSION

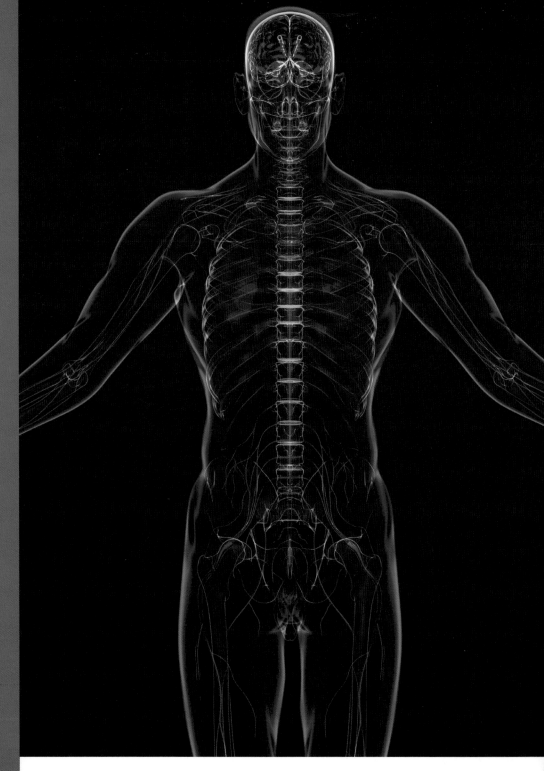

Your brain is your body's command center. It's involved with pretty much every-thing you do and feel.

When there's just too much on your to-do list, your body and brain will do their best to cope—but after a while, stress takes its toll.

deal with schoolwork, sports, relationships, and jobs. These aren't life-threatening situations—but they can take the same toll on your body as if they were. Here's what's going on inside your brain and body every time you feel stressed.

YOUR BODY'S COMMAND CENTER

Your brain is your body's command center. It takes in messages from the outside world and responds by sending out messages to the rest of your body. When it comes to stress reactions, certain areas of your brain are particularly important.

The hypothalamus is a part of the brain that's located near

STRESS AND TENSION

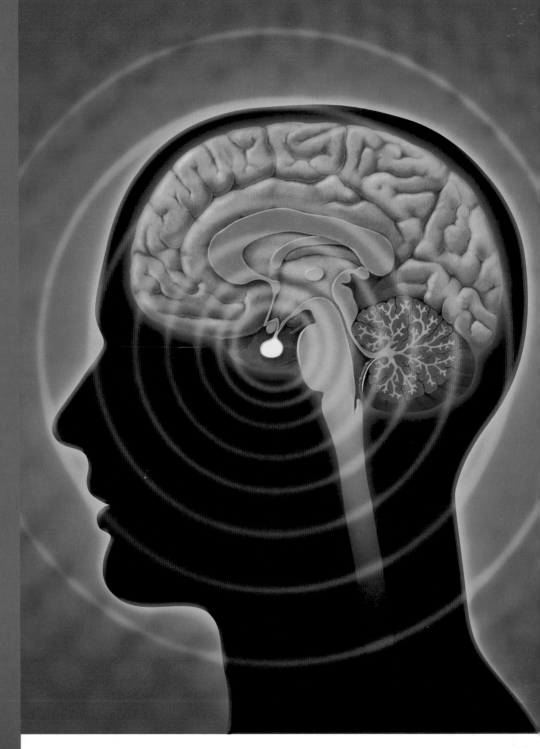

Your pituitary gland is a tiny little gland in your brain that controls a lot of your life.

Make Connections

If the adrenal glands' hormones are out of whack, they can cause serious diseases. Just a little bit more dopamine in your body, for example, can tighten blood vessels and cause high blood pressure. A shift in epinephrine might bring on an asthma attack, by constricting tiny airways in the lungs, or it could change the way your body processes sugar and cause diabetes. If the adrenal gland slacks off on cortisol production, you might end up with obesity, heart disease, or osteoporosis. Too much cortisol can contribute to some of the effects of aging, like baldness in men or memory loss.

where the spine runs into the skull. The hypothalamus sends out signals to the nearby pituitary gland, as well as the adrenal glands, which are much lower in your body, right above the kidneys. This connection between the hypothalamus, the pituitary gland, and the adrenal glands controls a whole bunch of very basic body functions. Among many other things, it regulates blood pressure, heart rate, body temperature, sleep patterns, reproduction, and hunger and thirst.

Obviously, your hypothalamus has a big job—but it's only about the size of a grape! It does its work by releasing two types of signaling chemicals called hormones. These hormones tell your pituitary and adrenal glands to either release their own sets of hormones—or to hold off from releasing any hormones.

The pituitary gland looks a little like a cherry hanging from a stem attached to the hypothalamus. It waits to receive instructions from the hypothalamus about which of its many hormones it should release—and how much of it to release when it does. The pituitary gland controls a lot of your life. It releases substances that regulate growth, sex, skin color, bone length, and muscle strength.

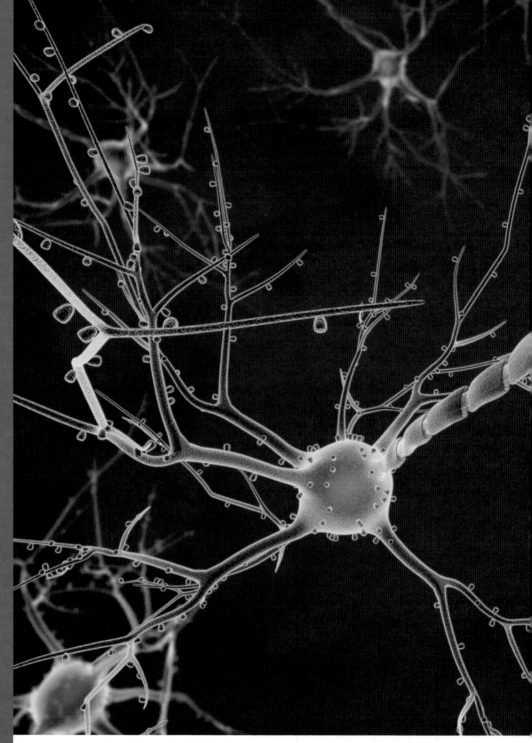

A neuron is an odd-looking cell with lots of spidery looking pieces called dendrites. Messages pass from one neuron's dendrites to another's—but the dendrites from two cells never quite touch. Neurotransmitters are necessary to carry signals across those tiny little gaps.

Make Connections

The brain is made up of billions of tiny cells called neurons. You also have billions more neurons throughout your body. These cells are sending messages to each other all the time, which is what allows you to think, move, and sense things. It's called your nervous system. Your nervous system picks up messages from the outside world through your various senses. Neurons carry these messages to your brain. Your brain makes sense of the various messages—it puts them together in a way you can understand—and then it sends out other messages back through the neurons, which tell your body to move or respond in various ways.

Neurons use chemicals to carry all these messages from one to the other. But each tiny nerve cell doesn't quite touch the one next to it. There's a little gap—called a synapse—between each set of neurons that are exchanging messages. Neurotransmitters are chemicals that carry messages across these tiny gaps. Without them, the message would never get to the next neuron.

There are dozens of kinds of neurotransmitters, and many play important roles in the feelings we call emotions.

Stress makes the hypothalamus start communicating in a unique way with the pituitary. Next, the pituitary sends a special hormone to the adrenal glands—and the adrenal glands do their part by manufacturing and releasing hormones called dopamine, epinephrine (also known as adrenaline), norepinephrine (also called noradrenaline), and cortisol. These hormones will affect basic body functions, like blood flow and breathing. In fact, even the tiniest amounts can make your body respond in big ways.

HORMONES AND STRESS

Say you're driving for the first time on icy roads, and you're fighting to keep the car from sliding into the ditch or into oncoming

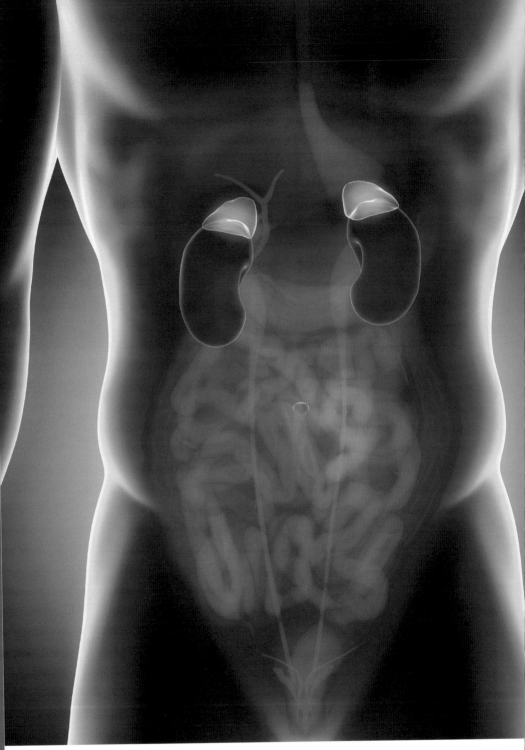

Your adrenal glands sit on top your kidneys. These glands produce many of the stress hormones that will bring about other changes in your body.

traffic. Sensing danger, the hypothalamus shoots out a hormone that prompts the pituitary gland to release another hormone called adrenocorticotropin (ACTH). Carried in the bloodstream to the adrenal glands, ACTH triggers the production of still other hormones, cortisol and epinephrine. These two hormones do their job, and now your body is surging with blood sugar, your heart is pounding, and your blood pressure soars. Your hands grip the steering wheel, and you manage to make it home safely.

That's a good thing—but problems arise when you start experiencing chronic stress. These same hormones can upset your body's normal functions. For example, cortisol directly impacts the storage of short-term memories in another part of your brain, the hippocampus. The stress hormones dopamine and epinephrine act as well on many of the networks within your brain, which in turn will affect your emotions. **Researchers** have also discovered that stress changes another neurotransmitter, serotonin. Serotonin plays an important role in our feelings of happiness and sadness, so when it's not in balance, you can end up feeling depressed. This explains why people who are chronically stressed are more prone to depression. Serotonin levels also affect aggression—which in turn explains why you're more likely to snap at your mother or get in a fight with your friend when you're going through a lot of stress.

STRESS AND DISEASE

Researchers are very interested in the ways that stress hormones affect our brains and bodies. Scientific studies are helping scientists and doctors understand the ways that chronic stress and tension can cause illnesses.

For example, epinephrine, one of the hormones released by the adrenal glands in response to stress, tells the cells responsible for repairing blood vessels to produce large quantities of a substance called ATP. Studies have found that in large amounts, ATP can trigger a heart attack or **stroke** by causing blood vessels to

To learn more about stress and the fight-or-flight response, scientists have studied parachute jumpers.

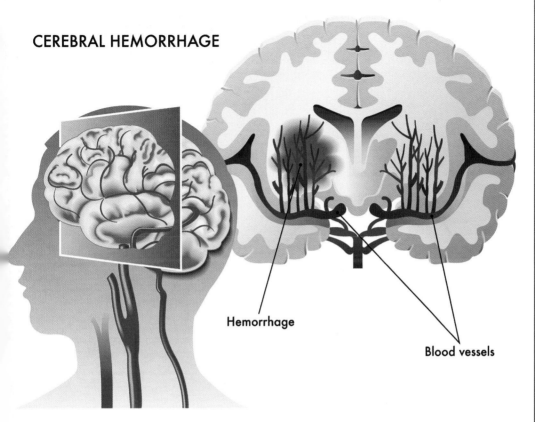

CEREBRAL HEMORRHAGE

Hemorrhage

Blood vessels

A stroke is when the blood vessels in your brain break and bleed into your brain, damaging brain cells. Another name for this is a cerebral hemorrhage.

narrow too rapidly and cut off blood flow.

In another study, researchers kept track of parachute jumpers' hormones. Every time a parachute jumper gets ready to leap out of an airplane, chances are good his fight-or-flight responses are going full blast—and scientists wanted to understand how that affected the men in the study. The researchers found an 84 percent surge in nerve growth factor (NGF) among young men who were getting ready for their first jump, compared with nonjumpers. Up to six hours after they hit ground, the jumpers' NGF levels were

STRESS AND TENSION

If you're stressed, you'll be more likely to catch a cold!

even higher—107 percent higher than in nonjumping men. Released by the pituitary gland as part of the stress response, NGF does good things for the body—but it is also attracted like a magnet to disease-fighting cells, where it hinders their ability to ward off infections. This helps explain how stress reactions can increase people's **susceptibility** to colds and even more serious illnesses, such as cancer.

A scientist named Dr. Sheldon Cohen, a professor of psychology at Carnegie Mellon University, did more research into stress and the immune system. He gave four hundred people a questionnaire to help him determine how much stress each person was experiencing. He then exposed each person in his study to nose drops containing cold viruses. About 90 percent of the stressed subjects (versus 74 percent of those not under stress) caught a cold. He also found that the stressed people had higher levels of a hormone called corticotrophin-releasing factor (CRF). "We know that CRF interferes with the immune system," Dr. Cohen explained. "That is likely the physical explanation why people under stress are more likely to catch a cold."

Stress hormones may also play a role in rheumatoid arthritis, a disease that makes joints sore and stiff. The hormone prolactin, released by the pituitary gland in response to stress, triggers cells that cause swelling in joints. In a study of a hundred people with rheumatoid arthritis, Dr. Kathleen S. Matt and other scientists from Arizona State University found that levels of prolactin were twice as high among people who said they had high levels of **interpersonal** stress as it was among people who said they were not stressed. Other studies have shown that prolactin tends to collect in people's joints, where it leads to swelling, pain, tenderness. "This is clearly what people mean when they say stress is worsening their arthritis," Dr. Matt said.

Researchers have also found that stress can make you feel pain more intensely than you would in the same circumstances if you weren't stressed. Endorphins are chemicals that help your body handle pain. They're sort of like natural pain relievers. When the pituitary gland releases the stress hormone ACTH, however, it hinders your body's production of endorphins. This can make you experience a sense of physical discomfort—and if you're already hurting for some reason (maybe you've just been to the dentist, for example, or you twisted your ankle during basketball practice), stress can make the pain seem worse.

A COMPLICATED REACTION

Scientists are working hard to understand stress reactions better, but there's a lot that's still a mystery. Not everyone who's stressed gets sick or depressed. Some people seem to be able to take stress in their stride, while others can't. It's a complicated reaction, with lots of factors playing their part in how we respond to stress. *Genetics* may play a role, meaning that some people may have inherited traits from their parents that help them naturally respond to stress more easily than others. Environment—how we're raised, where we live, all the circumstances of our lives—also plays a

Text-Dependent Questions

1. Where and what is your hypothalamus? What does it do?

2. Explain the connection between your hypothalamus, your pituitary gland, and your adrenal glands.

3. Discuss the effects of chronic stress on brain chemicals, as described in this chapter.

4. Describe how neurons send messages throughout your body.

5. Explain the findings of the research study done by Dr. Sheldon Cohen and what they indicate about stress's effects on the body.

6. Define "endorphins" and explain how stress affects them.

role. Researchers are even discovering that our past experiences of stress can change the way we respond to stress in the future.

Words to Understand

sensitized: Became more affected by something.

magnitude: How powerful or serious something is.

circuitry: A collection of electric systems that works together. These might be electric circuits like the ones that power your lights, or they might be the neurons that your brain is made of.

capacities: Abilities or powers to do something.

neurologist: A doctor or scientist who studies the brain and nerves.

cardiovascular systems: The systems in people's bodies that are made up of the heart and blood vessels.

variables: Anything that can change the final outcome of something.

THREE

How Does Stress Change Our Lives?

Stress is nothing new. It's a natural part of human life, and it always has been. However, some of us may not be coping very well with our lives' normal stress. When that happens, stress can become even more damaging to our well-being.

STRESS AS AN ALLERGY

When you have an allergic reaction to something, you may not respond all that strongly the first time you're exposed to whatever it is. Say you've never been around a cat until a friend of yours gets a kitten. The first time you pet the cat, you notice that your eyes are a little watery and your nose starts to drip. It doesn't really bother you, though, and you don't think much about it. You don't spend a lot of time at your friend's house, and you soon forget all about it. A few months later, though, you spend the night at your

Emotions
Alienation
Irritability
Apathy
Low Confidence

Behaviour
Accident Prone
Loss of Appetite
Restless
Smoking and Alcohol

Mind
Anxiety
Hasty Decisions
Negativity
Impaired Judgment

Body
Headaches
Skin Problems
Breathless

Stress

Stress brings with it a collection of symptoms—and the more stress you experience, the greater those symptoms become, to the point that they're like an allergic reaction to stress.

Make Connections

Experts have found that outward expressions of emotions (body language) mean different things in different cultures. For example, if a young person avoids looking directly at a person in authority, it is taken as a sign of respect in some cultures—but in other cultures, this expression suggests guilt or shame. A study of Chinese and Westerners also found that Chinese people are more likely to rely on others' eyes to judge their emotions, while Westerners pay more attention to eyebrows and mouths.

friend's house, and the cat sleeps on your bed. You wake up in the night feeling like you can't breathe. Your eyes are swollen, and your nose is plugged up. You're definitely allergic to cats!

As scientists continue to study the effects that stress has on our lives, they've discovered that we may respond to stress in a way that's a little like an allergy. The first time we run into something stressful in life, our bodies cope with it. But the more stress we experience, the more sensitive we may become to it. Once that happens, even the smallest stress can set off the chemical reactions in our brains and bodies that can prove to be so destructive in the long run. We've become allergic to stress!

But here's the weird thing—a person who's become *sensitized* to stress probably doesn't realize that her body's going into stress overdrive every time she encounters something stressful. With the conscious, rational part of her brain, she knows that the stress is no big deal—but the rest of her brain doesn't seem to realize that fact. Maybe she's late for class or she forgot her gym shorts—but her brain is responding as though her life was being threatened. According to one researcher, Dr. Michael Meaney of McGill University, "What happens is that sensitization leads the brain to

If you turn up the thermostat in your house, the heat will come on more often. In a similar way, when you've had too much stress in your life, your brain's "stress thermostat" gets turned up, so that it responds more often to even the smallest stresses.

Research Project

This chapter describes several research studies that investigated how stress affects people's lives. Using the library or the Internet, find another research study related to stress and describe its findings. Does it support or contradict the research included in this chapter?

re-circuit itself in response to stress. We know that what we are encountering may be a normal, everyday episode of stress, but the brain is signaling the body to respond inappropriately."

Another researcher, psychologist Jonathan C. Smith from the Stress Institute at Chicago's Roosevelt University, compared our bodies' stress reactions to a thermostat. Normally, the "thermostat" is set to respond at a level that matches the situation. The brain triggers the response that's appropriate for the crisis at hand, with major emergencies getting a far greater physical response than small mini-crises. But when we've encountered too much stress in the past, explained Dr. Smith, so that we've become over-sensitized to it, it's as though the thermostat has been turned up. Now the body responds to even small events—like being late for class or forgetting our gym shorts—as though they were major catastrophes.

PAST AND FUTURE STRESS

Scientists have also discovered that the age at which you begin experiencing stress can affect how well you handle it later in life. Young children who go through extreme stress—such as losing a parent, for example, or having an abusive caregiver—may find it more difficult to cope with stress as adults. Dr. Jean King, a

A serious trauma may change a child's brain, so that when he grows up, he's more sensitive to stress.

scientist at the University of Massachusetts Medical School, said, "What we now believe is that a stress of that *magnitude* occurring when you are young may permanently rewire the brain's *circuitry*, throwing the system askew and leaving it less able to handle normal, everyday stress." Dr. King went on to explain that this research proves the link between our emotions, our environment, and our physical responses.

Have you ever looked at someone and envied his ability to stay cool under pressure? Or have you ever heard someone described as "a rock," someone who remains calm and steady during a crisis? We tend to feel that people like this are stronger than other people. We might wish we could be as strong as they are. We may think to ourselves, "If only I had more self-control, if only I weren't so weak, I would handle life better." But the research shows that how we respond to stress has nothing to do with whether we're weak or strong. Instead, different people simply have different

Make Connections

Researchers investigate many aspects of human life and the world around us. When it comes to stress, scientific researchers aren't simply curious—they are hoping that by understanding the stress response, they may be able to develop medicine that will counteract the diseases that stress can cause. Dr. Smith from Roosevelt University said, "We may be able to develop drugs that can retune the entire neurochemical system. I think it's going to take years more research to better understand how an early trauma actually alters the neurochemical system. What is the mechanism by which psychological stress changes the way the brain communicates with the body? Does the same stress cause the same changes all the time? When are the developmental periods during which stress may be most harmful? As we continue to unveil the complex interactions between the mind and body, we may be able to isolate these reactions. That raises the possibility we can develop drugs to change them."

capacities for handling stress—and their capacities have a lot to do with what they've had to go through so far in life. In this case, trouble doesn't seem to make people stronger.

Stress can also cause physical problems far in the future from the original situation. Dr. Lawrence Brass, a **neurologist** at Yale Medical School, found that severe stress can make individuals more likely to have a stroke—even fifty years after the events that caused the original stress. Dr. Brass studied more than five hundred World War II veterans and found that the rate of stroke among those who had been prisoners of war (POWs) was eight times higher than among those veterans who had never been captured. At first, Dr. Brass thought his findings didn't make sense After all, the hormones that could help cause heart disease and

Make Connections

 Magnetic resonance imaging (MRI) is a test that uses a magnetic field and pulses of radio wave energy to make pictures of organs and structures inside the body. For an MRI test, the area of the body being studied is placed inside a special machine that contains a strong magnet. Pictures from an MRI scan are digital images that can be saved and stored on a computer for more study.

stroke are higher only for a few hours after a stressful event. "I began to realize we would have to take our understanding of stress farther," Dr. Brass said, "when I began to see that in some people stress can cause disease years after the initial event. The stress of being a POW was so severe it changed the way these folks responded to stress in the future—it sensitized them. . . . Years of this kind of hormonal assault may have weakened their *cardiovascular systems* and led to the strokes."

Another study, this one of child-abuse victims, used magnetic resonance imaging (MRI) to look inside the brains of thirty-eight women. Twenty of these women had a history of sexual abuse, while eighteen had never been abused. Among those women sexually abused as children, the researchers discovered, the hippocampus—a part of the brain that's important for storing memories—was smaller than normal. "What we are seeing," said Dr. Murray Stein of the University of California at San Diego, "is evidence that psychological stress can change the brain's makeup."

Scientists still can't predict exactly what effect stress will have on different people. There are many *variables* at work inside each person's brain, and we still don't know exactly how all those variables work together. Dr. Georgia Witkin, the director of the

Text-Dependent Questions

1. Explain how our reactions to stress could be similar to an allergic reaction.

2. Dr. Jonathan C. Smith compares our stress reaction to a thermostat. What does he mean?

3. Describe the two studies referred to in this chapter that indicate that stress can have long-term effects on people's bodies.

4. What is an MRI and what is it used for?

Stress Program at Mt. Sinai Medical Center in New York City, explained it like this: "No one thing is going to explain stress because there is not just one chemical reaction to stress. And it also does not mean that everyone who loses a parent or is the victim of a violent crime will suffer from stress the rest of his life. There are things about individuals—genetic susceptibilities, pre-existing medical conditions, the environment they were brought up in, . . . that must all be factored in. But the first pieces of the puzzle are being put into place."

How do you cope with stress? Does the littlest thing freak you out? Or are you one of those people who stays cool under pressure? Chances are you're somewhere in between—but no matter how you react to stress now, you can learn better ways to handle it in the future. While scientists are working hard to explain what happens inside your body when you're stressed and tense, psychologists have already developed strategies that will help you cope with life's stress a little better.

COPING STRATEGIES

Words to Understand

mastery: The skill or knowledge that makes you feel in control of a particular area of life.

FOUR

How Can We Learn to Cope with Stress?

Remember Jenna who was having such a stressful week? Her friend Abby told her, "You'll be fine. You're just stressed out. Relax!" What do you think? Was this helpful advice?

Well on the one hand, Abby's advice may have helped Jenna recognize that she was experiencing stress. Sometimes, we get so busy, we don't have time to think about what's going on in our lives. Just coping with everything we have to do takes all our attention, so that we don't have a chance to step back and understand why we may feel so awful right now. So when Abby pointed out the stress in Jenna's life, it may have helped Jenna to be more patient with herself. If Jenna understands how stress affects her body, she may even be able to take steps to counteract those effects.

Stress can seem like a heavy ball you can't put down—but there are strategies that will help you let your "stress ball" bounce away.

A toolbox contains lots of different tools. Each one works in a particular way; you don't try to hammer a nail with a tape measure, for example. Your toolbox of stress strategies will also contain different tools; some will work better in some circumstances than others.

But just being told, "Relax!" isn't much help when we're stressed. We need to have a "toolbox" of practical strategies for coping with stress. Experts tell us it's a good idea to have that toolbox ready *before* we're in a stressful situation. Once we're stressed, it's hard for our brains to focus. We'll do better if we have our toolbox already in place, so we can just reach in and pull out the tool that will help us most.

STRESS STRATEGIES

Here are a few strategies for managing stress you might want to keep handy. That way the next time you're stressed, you can try one out—and if one doesn't work, try another!

- **Progressive relaxation.** Curl your toes toward the soles of your feet as hard as you can for fifteen seconds and then

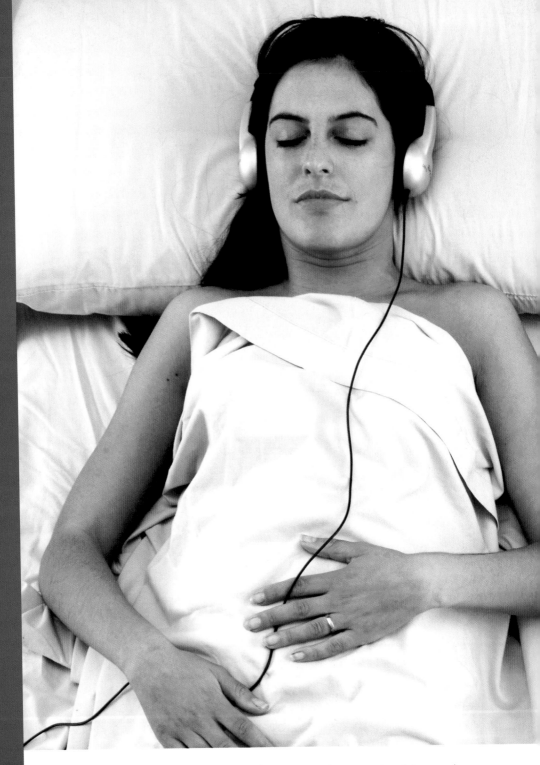

Listening to music may help you to relax your body's muscles.

Taking time to daydream can help you cope with stress. Each daydream is like a mini-vacation away from the stress of your current life.

relax them. One by one, tense and relax your muscles, working from your feet up to your legs, your stomach, your back, your shoulders, and your neck. When you are done, your entire body should be relaxed.

- **Visualization.** Imagine that you're somewhere calm and peaceful. This could be a real place or an imaginary one. Maybe you picture yourself sitting by the ocean or walking in a forest. Visualize everything about this place as clearly as possible. Feel the air on your face; listen to the wind in the trees or the sound of the waves. You may want to return to this same place whenever you feel stressed.

- **Free time.** Even on your busiest days, set aside twenty to thirty minutes a day to do anything you want, even if that's nothing at all. You may feel as though you can't possibly take the time, but chances are you're finding time to shower

Regular exercise makes you better able to cope with stress.

Make Connections

 Researchers have found that one of the effects that regular exercise has is that it reduces anxiety and depression. Experts believe that the reason exercise has this effect is that it increases the body's ability to respond to stress. It gives the body the chance to practice—and get better at—dealing with stress by forcing all the body's systems to communicate with each other more closely than usual. In other words, your cardiovascular system communications with your muscles, which communicate with your kidneys and digestive system, all of which is controlled by your nervous system. This workout of your body's communication system is one of the greatest benefits exercise gives you. And the less you exercise, researchers have found, the more poorly your body will respond to stress. It doesn't matter what kind of exercise you choose—just get out there and move!

and get dressed, no matter how busy you are. Consider this free time just as important!

- **Walk.** A brisk walk can help release some of the tension in your body. It can also help your brain chemistry go back to normal.

- **Music.** Music has a powerful effect on our brains and emotions. On your most stressful days, keep an iPod or some other device handy, loaded with whatever kind of music you find most relaxing.

- **Deep breathing.** Deep breathing exercises can be done in various ways. You might lie on the floor or on your bed and breathe deeply and slowly. Or you could sit in a

Physical
Activities
(Sports)

Meditation

Present
Moment
Awareness

Managing
Stress

Journaling
(Diary)

Leading
a Balanced
Life

Conflict
Resolution
Skills

The next time you feel stressed, remember to try a coping strategy!

reclining chair. Put a hand on your abdomen and a hand on your chest. As you breathe, make sure the hand on your abdomen is moving up and down rather than the one on your chest. Breathe slowly and deeply for five minutes, concentrating on the movement of each breath.

- **Meditate**. Meditation involves closing your eyes and focusing on your inner world. There are many meditation techniques, such as focusing on your breath, chanting a word or syllable, and using visualizations. Some people pray while they meditate. Some people simply withdraw their minds from the world around them. Scientists have found the meditation has powerful effects on brain chemistry.

- **Talk.** Talking with someone we trust can allow us to vent some of our tension, while at the same time helping us regain a better sense of perspective. The source of our stress may not seem so overwhelming once we've talked it out. The other person may also be able to point out helpful steps we could take to deal with the situation.

- **Lists.** If you make a list of small, doable things you need to accomplish each day, it will give you a sense of **mastery** at the end of the day when you can see how many things you've checked off. Feeling like you have a little more control over your life will help reduce your sense of stress.

- **Sleep.** When you're stressed, you may have difficulty sleeping at night, but do your best to get at least eight hours of sleep a night. Sleep is the body's way of renewing itself, and getting enough sleep will help you cope with stress better. Take short naps during the day if you're tired.

- **Say no.** If you're already stressed out and tense, don't agree to add responsibilities to your to-do list. If a friend

Sometimes the best strategy for coping with stress is to simply say no to any more stress entering your life. There's not time for everything!

You may feel as though a cup of coffee will help you relax and give you a shot of energy—but the caffeine in coffee can actually make your body's stress reactions even worse.

asks you to do a favor or a teacher suggests you join an after-school club, explain that you have a lot on your plate right now. Take a look at your schedule and see if there's something you could cut from it. Maybe you don't *have* to be quite as stressed as you are. It's okay to say no sometimes!

- **Avoid caffeine, alcohol, nicotine, junk food, and drugs.** It may be tempting to turn to these for some short-term relief when you're feeling stressed, but actually, the

Research Project

One of the strategies for coping with stress that this chapter suggests is meditation. Using the library or the Internet, find out more about meditation. Describe several different meditation techniques, including religious and non-religious approaches to meditation. Then do an experiment in your own life. First record your stress levels at the end of every day for two weeks, using a scale of 1 to 10. Then meditate every day for two weeks, and again record your stress level at the end of each day. Did your stress go down when you meditated?

chemicals in these substances will only make stress's harmful physical effects even worse.

- *Laugh.* Laughter is a great way to reduce tension and counteract stress. Cultivate your sense of humor. Find reasons to laugh every day. Don't take life so seriously!

- *Reasonable expectations.* Don't demand perfection of yourself or others. No one is perfect—and trying to achieve perfection just adds to your stress levels.

UNDERSTANDING STRESS

Psychologists have found that simply knowing about how stress affects the body can help people cope with it a little better. By being aware that we're stressed, we can stop blaming ourselves when we're not handling life as well as we do other times. We can give ourselves a break and look for ways to reduce our stress levels.

Text-Dependent Questions

1. Explain what a strategy is and why it's necessary for coping with stress.

2. Of the stress strategies suggested in this chapter, which three do you think would help you most the next time you're feeling stressed? Explain how each of these strategies could help you cope with stress.

3. What strategies suggested in this chapter do you think would be less helpful to you? Explain why, referring to what you've learned about stress in this book.

4. According to the sidebar in this chapter, how might exercise help us cope with stress?

So the next time life piles up on you, remember—you're not alone. People have been experiencing stress and tension for thousands of years. You're not crazy, and you're not a bad person. Stress and tension are real and normal.

Now go do something fun that will help you relax!

Find Out More

IN BOOKS

Biegel, Gina. *The Stress Reduction Workbook for Teens: Mindfulness Skills to Help You Deal with Stress.* Oakland, Calif.: Instant Help, 2010.

Bodhipaksa. *Mindfulness Meditations for Teens.* New Market, N.H.: Wildmind, 2011.

Elkin, Allen. *Stress Management for Dummies.* New York: For Dummies, 2013.

Hipp, Earl. *Fighting Invisible Tigers: Stress Management for Teens.* Minneapolis, Minn.: Free Spirit, 2013.

Kerr, Christiane. *Rays of Calm: Relaxation for Teenagers.* Borough Green, UK: Diviniti, 2007.

McKay, Matthew. *The Relaxation and Stress Reduction Workbook.* Oakland, Calif.: New Harbinger, 2008.

Moore, Tim. *Meditation.* New York: Rosen, 2008.

ONLINE

The Complete Guide to Understanding Your Emotions
www.psychologytoday.com/blog/fulfillment-any-age/201205/the-complete-guide-understanding-your-emotions

Developing Emotional Awareness
www.helpguide.org/toolkit/developing_emotional_awareness.htm

Understanding Emotions
www.trans4mind.com/heart/emotions.html

Understanding Emotions Without Words
www.sciencedaily.com/releases/2011/11/111102093045.htm

Understanding Your Emotions
www.wire.wisc.edu/yourself/Emotions/Understanding_emotions.
aspx

Series Glossary of Key Terms

adrenaline: An important body chemical that helps prepare your body for danger. Too much adrenaline can also cause stress and anxiety.

amygdala: An almond-shaped area within the brain where the flight-or-flight response takes place.

autonomic nervous system: The part of your nervous system that works without your conscious control, regulating body functions such as heartbeat, breathing, and digestion.

cognitive: Having to do with thinking and conscious mental activities.

cortex: The area of your brain where rational thinking takes place.

dopamine: A brain chemical that gives pleasure as a reward for certain activities.

endorphins: Brain chemicals that create feelings of happiness.

fight-or-flight response: Your brain's reaction to danger, which sends out messages to the rest of the body, getting it ready to either run away or fight.

hippocampus: Part of the brain's limbic system that plays an important role in memory.

hypothalamus: The brain structure that gets messages out to your body's autonomic nervous system, preparing it to face danger.

limbic system: The part of the brain where emotions are processed.

neurons: Nerve cells found in the brain, spinal cord, and throughout the body.

neurotransmitters: Chemicals that carry messages across the tiny gaps between nerve cells.

serotonin: A neurotransmitter that plays a role in happiness and depression.

stress: This feeling that life is just too much to handle can be triggered by anything that poses a threat to our well-being, including emotions, external events, and physical illnesses.

Index

About the Author & Consultant

Rosa Waters lives in New York State. She has worked as a writer for several years, producing works on health, history, and other topics.

Cindy Croft is director of the Center for Inclusive Child Care at Concordia University, St. Paul, Minnesota where she also serves as faculty in the College of Education. She is field faculty at the University of Minnesota Center for Early Education and Development program and teaches for the Minnesota on-line Eager To Learn program. She has her M.A. in education with early childhood emphasis. She has authored *The Six Keys: Strategies for Promoting Children's Mental Health in Early Childhood Programs* and co-authored *Children and Challenging Behavior: Making Inclusion Work* with Deborah Hewitt. She has worked in the early childhood field for the past twenty years.

Picture Credits

Fotolia.com:
8: olly
10: freshidea
12: ra2 studio
20: SCHMaster
22: SCHMaster
23: iQoncept
24: lom123
26: shumpc
28: CLIPAREA.com
30: goce risteski
31: rob3000
32: Tom Wang
36: Ariwasabi

38: Dmitry
40: JJ'Studio
42: ia_64
46: creative soul
48: kbuntu
49: Maksym Yemelyanov
50: gosphotodesign
51: Darren Baker
52: tomalu
54: Dmitry
56: rnl
57: vladimirfloyd

14: Solarseven | Dreamstime.com